MEXICO:
FACTS AND FIGURES

ELLYN SANNA

CIRCUITO INTERIOR ↑
← CHAPULTEPEC

RIO LERMA →

Mexico City is one of the largest cities in the world; together with its suburbs, it is home to more than 20 million people.

OUR
SOUTHERN NEIGHBOR
MEXICO

MEXICO:
FACTS AND FIGURES

ELLYN SANNA

Mason Crest Publishers
Philadelphia

Mason Crest Publishers
370 Reed Road
Broomall PA 19008
www.masoncrest.com

First printing

1 3 5 7 9 8 6 4 2

Library of Congress Cataloging-in-Publication Data on file at the Library of Congress

ISBN 1-59084-088-7

TABLE OF CONTENTS

OUR SOUTHERN NEIGHBOR MEXICO

Roger E. Hernández
Senior Consulting Editor

INTRODUCTION

Mexico is a country in the midst of great change. And what happens in Mexico will have an important impact on the United States, its neighbor to the north.

These changes are being put in place by President Vicente Fox, who was elected in 2000. For the previous 71 years, power had been held by presidents from one single party, known in Spanish as *Partido Revolucionario Institucional* (Institutional Revolutionary Party, or PRI). Some of those presidents have been accused of corruption. President Fox, from a different party called *Partido de Acción Nacional* (National Action Party, or PAN), says he wants to eliminate that corruption. He also wants to have a friendlier relationship with the United States, and for American businesses to increase trade with Mexico. That will create more jobs, he says, and decrease poverty—which in turn will mean fewer Mexicans will find themselves forced to emigrate in search of a better life.

But it would be wrong to think of Mexico as nothing more than a poor country. Mexico has given the world some of its greatest artists and writers. Carlos Fuentes is considered one of the greatest living novelists, and poet-essayist Octavio Paz was awarded the Nobel Prize for Literature in 1990, the most prestigious honor a writer can win. Painters such as Diego Rivera and José Clemente Orozco specialized in murals, huge paintings done on walls that tell of the history of the nation. Another famous Mexican painter, Rufino Tamayo, blended the "cubist" style of modern European painters like Picasso with native folk themes.

Tamayo's paintings in many ways symbolize what Mexico is: A blend of the culture of Europe (more specifically, its Spanish version) and the indigenous cultures that predated the arrival of Columbus.

Those cultures were thriving even 3,000 years ago, when the Olmec people built imposing monuments that survive to this day in what are now the states of Tabasco and Veracruz. Later and further to the south in the Yucatán Peninsula, the Maya civilization flourished. They constructed cities in the midst of the jungle, complete with huge temples, courts in which ball games were played, and highly accurate calendars intricately carved in stone pillars. For some mysterious reason, the Mayans abandoned most of these great centers 1,100 years ago.

The Toltecs, in central Mexico, were the next major civilization. They were followed by the Aztecs. It was the Aztecs who built the city of Tenochitlán in the middle of a lake in what is now Mexico City, with long causeways connecting it to the mainland. By the early 1500s it was one of the largest cities anywhere, with perhaps 200,000 inhabitants.

Then the Spanish came. In 1519, twenty-seven years after Columbus arrived in the Americas, Hernán Cortés landed in Yucatán with just 600 soldiers plus a few cannons and horses. They marched inland, gaining allies as they went along among indigenous peoples who resented being ruled by the Aztecs. Within two years Cortés and the Spaniards ruled Mexico. They had conquered the Aztec Empire and devastated their great capital.

It was in that destruction that modern Mexico was born. The influence of the Aztecs and other indigenous people did not disappear even though untold numbers were killed. But neither can Mexico be recognized today without the Spanish influence.

Spain ruled for three centuries. Then in 1810 Mexicans began a struggle for independence from colonial Spain, much like the United States had fought for its own independence from Great Britain. In 1821 Mexico finally became an independent nation.

The newly born republic faced many difficulties. There was much poverty, especially among descendants of indigenous peoples; most of the wealth and political power was in the hands of a small elite of Spanish ancestry. To make things worse, Mexico lost almost half of its territory to the United States in a war that lasted from 1846 to 1848. Many still resent the loss of territory, which accounts for lingering anti-American sentiments among some Mexicans. The country was later occupied by France, but under national hero Benito Juárez Mexico regained its independence in 1867.

The next turning point in Mexican history came in 1911, when a revolution meant to help the millions of Mexicans stuck in poverty began against dictator Porfirio Díaz. There was violence and fighting until 1929, when Plutarco Elías Calles founded what was to become the *Partido Revolucionario Institucional*. It brought stability as well as economic progress. Yet millions of Mexicans remained in poverty, and as time went on PRI rulers became increasingly corrupt.

It was the desire of the people of Mexico to trust someone other than the candidate of PRI that resulted in the election of Fox. And so this nation of more than 100 million, with its ancient heritage, its diverse mestizo culture, its grinding poverty, and its glorious arts, stands on the brink of a new era. Modern Mexico is seeking a place as the leader of all Latin America, an ally of the United States, and an important voice in global politics. For that to happen, Mexico must narrow the gap between the rich and poor and bring more people in the middle class. It will be interesting to watch as Fox and the Mexican people work to bring their country into the first rank of nations.

A train runs along Copper Canyon, in the Sierra Madre mountain range of Chihuahua. Copper Canyon is four times as large as Arizona's Grand Canyon, and is almost 300 feet (about 90 meters) deeper than the Grand Canyon.

1

MEXICO TODAY

Today's Mexico is a mixture of many things. Ancient traditions contrast with modern technology; Indian traditions and languages mingle with Spanish customs; Catholicism blends with native religions; and poverty and wealth live side by side. Even the people are a combination of European and Indian descent.

Mexicans today are proud of their rich heritage and their beautiful land—but they also know that their nation has many problems. Wealth is not spread evenly among all members of the population; the rich are very rich, but the poor are very poor—and unfortunately, there are more poor people in Mexico than there are rich people. The nation's economy has suffered for centuries, contributing to problems like poor health care, unemployment, illiteracy, and crime. Mexico also depends on its oil industry for much of its wealth; this means that its finances are linked too closely with the worldwide price of oil. When oil prices sink, so does Mexico's economy.

As the southernmost nation in North America, Mexico is tied to both the United States to the north and the other Latin American countries to the south. Mexico shares the language, heritage, and customs of much of Latin America—but it also has close emotional and economic bonds with its northern neighbor. Living so close to the United States, Mexicans see the wealth and opportunities enjoyed by many Americans. They want these same benefits for themselves, and as a result, some Mexicans rebel against their own government, while many others leave Mexico all together and *immigrate* to the United States, hoping to find a better life there. Many Mexicans enter America illegally; if they are caught, they will be sent back to Mexico.

Ejidos are lands that are jointly owned by a group of citizens. Initially, this was the process that the Indians used, but even today over 55 percent of the property of Mexico is owned in this way. The ejidos typically consist of farmland, pastures, and a small township. The land is owned communally, but each family has a section that they can work independently. This process works well, for most citizens cannot afford large areas of land privately. Owned jointly and passed through generations of families, it is an affordable way to live.

As Mexico enters the 21st century, its president, Vicente Fox, is working with the U.S. government to find solutions to some of Mexico's many problems, including illegal immigration, drug trafficking, and environmental issues. The U.S. government estimates that as much as half of the heroin and marijuana and most of the cocaine entering the United States come either from Mexico or through it. The problem straddles the border, for while the drugs may come from Mexico, the demand for them in America ensures that they will continue to be smuggled across the border. By the same token, Mexico and the United States

Archaeologists look for clues to Mexico's past civilizations, excavating an ancient city called Milta near Monte Alban, Oaxaca. A church from the Spanish colonial period stands in the background.

need to work together to clean up the air and water they both share. The two governments are working to find solutions, but distrust exists on both sides.

For centuries, Mexico's weak economy has been its most serious dilemma, since so many of its other troubles stem from this basic problem. Recently, however, the outlook for the Mexican economy looks more hopeful. Vicente Fox, the first president to be elected from a more progressive political party, hopes to balance the budget, reduce *inflation*, decrease dependency on the oil industry, and encourage foreign investment in Mexico's other industries.

Mexican children wear colorful costumes for a pre-Lenten festival at San Patricio-Melaqúe, near Manzanillo.

The North American Trade Agreement (NAFTA) is one of the key factors in Mexico's current economic growth. This agreement between the United States, Canada, and Mexico removes trade restrictions between the participating countries. This means that the countries do not have to pay taxes when they sell products from one country to another. It provides businesses with more opportunities for investment, while it encourages cooperation between nations.

Under NAFTA, *maquiladoras* have thrived. These are Mexican factories owned by foreign companies that *import* the materials needed for manufacturing and then *export* the finished products, all without having to pay any taxes. For example, fabric and sewing machines might be brought from the United States into Mexico, where they would be used to manufacture t-shirts in a *maquiladora*; the t-shirts would then be sent back to the United States. *Maquiladoras* manufacture mostly electronics, clothing, and cars. By 1999, more than 3,500 of these plants employed about 1.2 million workers.

Maquiladoras help U.S. businesses make large profits, since companies do not have to pay their workers U.S. wages; in fact, some workers make as little as 75 cents an hour. The businesses also do not have to obey the expensive safety regulations with which they would have to comply if the factory was located within the United States. And it is cheap and easy to ship the goods back to the American market.

There is a growing international concern, however, that the laborers in *maquiladoras* are receiving unfair wages while they work in an environment that is often unsafe. Nevertheless, the system does bring foreign money into Mexico, and it helps create jobs that are desperately needed.

But Mexico is far more than merely its government or its problems. Mexico is made up of people, people who are artistic, resourceful, and loving. Their strong sense of identity was forged in the fires of Mexico's long history, and that history now inspires the Mexican people to face the future with hope.

2

THE HISTORY OF MEXICO

More than 3,000 years ago, the Olmec civilization flourished in the land that is now Mexico. These ancient people built cultural centers and left their artwork as reminders to today's world. They were followed by many other great cultures: the Teotihuacán civilization, then the Mayan, and finally the Aztec. By the early 16th century, the Aztecs ruled most of Mexico with a cruel hand.

When Hernán Cortés arrived in Mexico, looking to claim this land for Spain, many of the people ruled by the Aztecs were eager to join forces with him. They resented the Aztecs' rule, and they hoped that with the help of the Spanish they could be free at last. Meanwhile, the Aztec ruler, Montezuma II, mistook Cortés for one of the Aztecs' favorite gods, Quetzacoatl. Montezuma opened his kingdom to the

This large sculpture, called a Chac Mool, represents a Toltec rain god. The Toltecs were one of many native groups that have lived and established civilizations in Mexico over the past 3,000 years.

white strangers—and the Spanish repaid him by taking him hostage and eventually slaughtering many of his people.

In the 300 years that followed, Mexico's native peoples suffered under Spain's rule. Many of them died after being exposed to diseases like **smallpox**, for which they had no **immunities**. The Spanish put them to work on their **haciendas**, tried to take away their culture and religion, and refused to give them any voice in their government.

At last, in 1810, Father Miguel Hidalgo encouraged the native Mexicans to revolt against their Spanish rulers. Their battle failed, but the fight for independence could not be stopped. In 1821, Mexico at last won its freedom from Spain.

The years that followed, however, were full of turmoil for the nation. One leader after another took control of Mexico and then was overthrown. In the aftermath of the Mexican-American War, Mexico lost much of its northern territories to the United States.

In 1861, Benito Juárez, of Indian descent, became president, and the country's fortunes took a turn for the better. Then, in 1863, the French invaded Mexico and made the Archduke Maximilian its emperor. Maximilian and his wife Carlota came to love the Mexican people, but they did not return his feelings. Four years later, Juárez drove the French out, executed Maximilian, and resumed his presidency.

Between 1877 and 1911, however, Porfirio Díaz ruled the country. Although Díaz did work to build his nation's economy, under his rule the rich only got richer while the poor became poorer yet. In 1910, Francisco Madero called for a revolution against the Díaz dictatorship. Rebels Pancho Villa and Emiliano Zapatoa joined forces with Madero,

Dancers wearing the costumes and using the musical instruments of the ancient Aztecs perform on the Zocolo, in the heart of Mexico City.

and together they brought an end to the era in Mexico's history known as the Porfiriato.

The years that followed were still more troubled. Between 1913 and 1920, 10 different presidents ruled the nation, as revolutionary and counter-revolutionary forces battled each other. Finally, in 1920, Álvaro Obregón became president. His government brought an end to the revolution and ushered in the modern era in Mexican history.

The years since then, however, have been far from peaceful. The Institutional Revolutionary Party (PRI) controlled politics, but under their leadership, the gap between the rich and the poor continued to widen. In 1968, before the Summer Olympics were scheduled to be held in Mexico City, the tension lead to a student strike that quickly turned

Pedestrians walk past the enormous sculpted heads of three 19th-century Mexican patriots—Benito Juárez, Miguel Hidalgo, and Venustiano Carranza—in Ensenada, Baja California.

into a riot. Several students were killed, and international attention turned to Mexico's problems.

In 1970 the discovery of new oil reserves combined with the rising prices of oil to give Mexico's economy a much-needed boost. However, the nation's leaders again made foolish choices that plunged their country's economy into still deeper hot water. As the *peso* was devalued in the early 1980s, the nation found itself in the midst of an ever-worsening economic crisis.

Internal rebellion and international help has driven Mexico's leaders to seek solutions for their nation's desperate problems. Scandals involving the PRI have weakened the controlling political party, and in 1997, the PRI finally lost its majority in the government. In 2000, Vicente Fox was elected. He is the first non-PRI president in 70 years, and the nation looks to his leadership with hope.

A river flows peacefully through San Ignacio, Baja California. This Mexican state borders California in the United States.

3

THE STATES

Mexico's 31 states and capital city make up a land of rich diversity. The geography of this land is as varied as its people, for it contains deserts and *tropical* jungles, beaches and mountains, lava fields and deep-sea fishing resorts. The land is sprinkled with ancient archeological wonders, ethnic festivals, and world-famous art. No wonder Mexico is a favorite vacation spot for so many people.

BAJA CALIFORNIA

If you were to enter Mexico at its most western northern border, directly below San Diego, California, you would find yourself in the Mexican state of Baja California. Tijuana is the border city that would give you your first glimpse of Mexican culture.

Tijuana, however, is like no other Mexican city. Although it is only the fourth largest Mexican city, it boasts the largest growth rate in the country. Mexicans from all over the country come to Tijuana, hoping to find a job in the many factories that send their wastes into the air and land around the city. Tijuana is dirty and not very pretty; there is not enough housing for the flocks of people that have come looking for work, and many make do with shacks built from discarded packing crates, pieces of metal, and even cardboard boxes. Americans from across the border also crowd the streets of Tijuana, shopping for cheap Mexican crafts or looking for a good time in Tijuana's noisy nightlife. Others come to watch a jai alai game or a bullfight, and still other Mexicans come to Tijuana to attend the top-notch Ibero-American University.

As you travel south from Tijuana, you will find yourself traveling down a long, narrow peninsula that reaches down between the Pacific Ocean and the Gulf of California. The land around you is dry and mountainous, and once you leave Tijuana's busy streets behind, the population is scarce, and the communities are small.

MEXICO: FACTS AND FIGURES

Total area: 755,866 sq. miles
(1,958,201 sq. km)

Population: 100 million

Population growth rate: 2.3 percent

Urban population: 74 percent (2002)

Literacy rate: 89 percent (2002)

Income per capita: US$3,611 (2000)

BAJA CALIFORNIA SUR

A little less than halfway down the peninsula, you will find yourself crossing the state border into Baja California Sur. This state is much like its closest neighbor to the north, but it has even fewer people. There are, however, a few cities, and these are far different from sprawling, dirty Tijuana.

Guerrero Negro is the first city just across the border. The town was founded in 1937 when a North American company began extracting and exporting salt from

The desert stretches across Baja California Sur, the least densely populated Mexican state.

the nearby *lagoon*. Even the air tastes salty in Guerrero Negro, and the salt plant there is the world's largest. It produces over 6 million tons of salt a year. But one of the most fascinating events that takes place in Guerrero Negro has to do with whales rather than salt. Each year, between 10,000 and 20,000 gray whales come here, *migrating* as many as 6,000 miles from Alaska in the north. The whales come here to play and give birth to their young in Guerrero Negro's calm, warm lagoons.

Closer to the tip of Baja California's peninsula is the city of La Paz, the capital of Baja California Sur. Although the city's name means "the peace," the city has a long history of struggles. Its isolation made life hard for the settlers who tried to live there in the 1700s and 1800s. In the 18th century, disease wiped out much of the human population— and then in the 19th century other diseases attacked the oyster population in the neighboring bay, destroying the pearl industry that had once thrived there. Today, though, many tourists come to this city to enjoy the beautiful beaches and sport fishing. La Paz has found its peace at last.

26

SINALOA

From La Paz, you can take a ferry across the Gulf of California to the mainland. When you land, you will find yourself in Sinaloa, a long, narrow state that is sandwiched between the gulf and the foothills of the Sierra Madre Occidental. Like Baja California, Sinaloa has desert lands, but unlike the rocky peninsula, this state also has fertile valleys and mountainsides where thick vegetation thrives. The state has four main rivers—the Fuerte, the Sinaloa, the Mocorito, and the Piaxtla— and these supply the land with surface water. With the help of irrigation, the state produces farm products for Mexico, especially mangos, cotton, and sugarcane. It also has the largest canning factory in Latin America.

One of Sinaloa's main cities is Mazatlán. This is Mexico's chief Pacific port, and the country's largest shrimp fleet docks there. The residents of the city enjoy baseball and bullfights, while visitors love the beaches. For a sufficient tip from tourists, cliff divers will leap 40 to 50 feet into water below.

The capital of Sinaloa is Culiacan, an agricultural center. It is one of the oldest cities in Mexico; archeological evidence indicates that people lived there as early as A.D. 900, while the present city was founded by the Spanish in 1531. Despite its long history, however, the city attracts few tourists, and today it is modern and urban.

SONORA

If you were to travel north along the Gulf of California from Sinaloa, you would find yourself entering the state of Sonora. In terms of land area, Sonora is the second-largest state in Mexico, and its population is growing as well. Like Baja California Norte, Sonora is located on the U.S.-Mexican border, which means that it is attractive to American industries looking to set up factories inside Mexico's borders. Big companies like Ford Motor Company, AT&T, Pepsico, Velcro USA, IBM, ITT Power Systems, and Sara Lee manufacture from within Sonora. As a result of so much foreign investment, the state is Mexico's leading producer of electronic equipment, plastics, and chemical products.

Most of these factories are focused around Hermosilla, Sonora's capital. Although the city is not as close to the U.S. border as other communities, the city government has worked hard at attracting foreign companies. The city was first founded in 1700 as a military base for the Spaniards who were battling the Native Americans, and the old fort still stands at the heart of the city.

Around Hermosilla lies fertile farmland. Irrigation projects have brought water to the desert land, and wheat, corn, cotton, pecans, oranges, and grapes flourish under the warm sun. Although the Sonora Desert, the third largest desert in North America, stretches across much of the state, *reclamation* projects take advantage of the state's Yaqui, Sonora, and Mayo Rivers, opening up still more farmland for use.

Mexico's form of government is a presidential republic with a federal structure. The head of state is elected by a nationwide vote for a six-year term. Legislative power is exercised by a congress composed of the senate and the chamber of deputies. Estados Unidos Mexicanos (the United Mexican States) includes 31 states and the Federal District, which contains the capital, Mexico City.

CHIHUAHUA

Sonora's neighbor to the east is the state of Chihuahua, Mexico's largest state. To the north, Chihuahua is bordered by New Mexico and Texas. The Río Grande is Chihuahua's northeastern boundary line, separating it from the state of Texas.

Ciudad Juárez is the most important city on this boundary line. Like El Paso, its American sister city across the Río Grande, Juárez has grown in the valley carved out of the Rocky Mountains by the great river. Like Tijuana and other border towns, Juárez sees a lot of American tourists coming across to enjoy the wild party atmosphere. Other sections of the city are packed with factories, most owned by American firms that have relocated in Mexico to take advantage of the low production costs. The city was founded in 1581 by the Spanish, and the old sections of the city still exist.

If you cross the Chihuahuan Desert to the south of Juárez, eventually you will come to the state's capital, the city of Chihuahua. This city, founded in 1709, is the center for the state's mining operations and cattle raising. The lumber industry of the Sierra Madre mountains also contributes to much of the city's income. Although Chihuahua is exposed on the north to the desert's sandstorms, it also has rich pasturelands. During the Mexican Revolution, Pancho Villa had his headquarters here; his band of cowboys and bandits attacked the government of Porfirio Díaz from this base, and his home, Quinta Luz, is still one of the city's major attractions.

The official language of Mexico is Spanish, although many people speak the native Nahuatl and Maya languages.

The state of Chihuahua contains people as diverse as the land itself. In the 1920s, **Mennonites** from the United States were attracted here by the rich pastures, and today they still maintain their communities in Chihuahua's agricultural areas. Like the Mennonites, the Tarahumara people live in isolation from the rest of the world, but their ancient native culture is far different. The Tarahumara sell their crafts in Chihuahua's cities, and then retreat to their simple lifestyle in Chihuahua's Sierra Madre mountains.

DURANGO

South of the state of Chihuahua lies Durango, a rocky, mountainous state whose capital is the city of Durango. If you are a moviegoer, this city may look familiar to you: more than a hundred American, British, and Mexican films have been shot in the surrounding area. Many of the sets are still standing where John Wayne once hunted bandits in the desolate hills outside the city.

Although Durango makes money from the many movie sets that are scattered across this area, even more important are its rich natural resources. When the Spanish arrived in 1563, they discovered that gold, silver, lead, copper, and iron were hidden inside Durango's hills. One of the largest iron deposits in the world is just north of the city of Durango.

The wealth from these many mines can be seen in the city's huge cathedral and government buildings. The *Palacio de Gobierno* houses two of Mexico's great 20th-century **murals**, one by Francisco Montoya and the other by Ernesto Flores Esquivel.

Every July, the city of Durango celebrates for two weeks of *Feria Nacional*. The celebrations are wrapped around July 4, the day of the *Virgen del Refugio*, and July 22, the anniversary of Durango's birth in 1563. People come from all over the country to buy cows, bet on cockfights, and enjoy the good music and food.

ZACATECAS

As you continue your journey south, you will leave the state of Durango and enter Zacatecas, a state at the very center of Central Mexico's high desert. Although the land is dry, like Durango, it is rich with hidden minerals. Silver was once especially important to this area.

In the 1500s, a native Mexican gave a silver trinket to one of the early Spanish colonists, triggering a rush of hopeful miners to this area. The city of Zacatecas grew out of this boom. During the 300 years that Spain ruled Mexico, more than a billion dollars of silver and other precious metals were stripped from the mines of Zacatecas.

Benito Juárez and his troops defeated local rebels here in 1871, but during the Mexican Revolution, Pancho Villa and his rebel forces found victory in the hills of Zacatecas. Today, many of the silver mines have run dry, and the Revolution is long over, but the city of Zacatecas has kept its heritage of wealth and culture. Although not many tourists find their way to the center of Mexico, Zacatecas is well worth the trip. The streets are lined with colonial **baroque** architecture, and the city continues to be a haven for artists and intellectuals.

AGUASCALIENTES

If you leave Zacatecas behind and travel south, you will cross the border into the state of Aguascalientes ("warm waters"). The state is named after its fresh hot springs, but the Spanish first called the region *"perforada"* or "perforated" because of the **catacombs** and tunnels that the native people had built beneath the land.

The capital of this small state is the city of Aguascalientes, a huge and growing industrial city. Neither the state or the city has many attractions to bring tourists here, and as a result, travelers who do venture here often find that the people are unusually friendly and curious.

In April, however, people from around Mexico come to the city of Aguascalientes to celebrate the Feast of San Marcos. This month-long *fiesta* attracts artists, musicians, dancers, actors, and poets.

JALISCO

As you continue to travel south, you will enter the much larger state of Jalisco. Unlike the central states through which you've just traveled, Jalisco is bordered to the west by the Pacific Ocean. Lake Chapala, Mexico's second largest lake, also lies within its borders, and the Río Grande de Santiago flows out of the lake and across the state, providing the state with moisture.

MAJOR CITIES IN MEXICO AND THEIR POPULATIONS

Mexico City, 20 million
Guadalajara, 3.5 million
Monterrey, 3.1 million
Puebla de Zaragoza, 1.4 million
León de los Aldamas, 1.1 million
Ciudad Juárez, 797,679
Mérida, 557,340
San Luis Potosí, 525,819
Torreón, 459,809

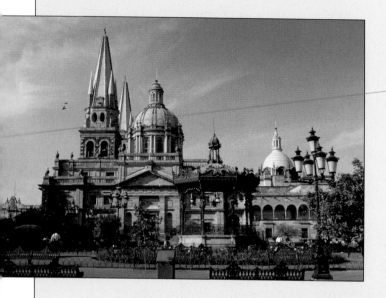

The cathedral of Guadalajara is one of the finest buildings in Mexico. Guadalajara is the capital of Jalisco, and the second-largest city in Mexico.

The state's capital and largest city is Guadalajara. This city was first founded by one of the most brutal of the Spanish *conquistadors*, a man named Nuño de Guzman. De Guzman killed so many of the Indians in the area that very little of the native culture survived. In the 19th century, when wealthy Mexicans wanted to escape the political unrest in Mexico City, they fled to Guadalajara, and here they surrounded themselves with a distinctive Spanish culture. The symbols of that culture—tequila, *mariachi* music, and the *hat dance*—have become important to the entire nation. Today, the city is Mexico's second largest. Although it has growing industries, it also still has its stately colonial architecture and fine museums.

Jalisco's many villages attract tourists with their colorful markets and quaint handicrafts. Tourists are also drawn to one of Jalisco's coastal cities, Puerto Vallarta. Visitors find here luxurious resorts and wide, clean beaches.

NAYARIT

If you make a quick trip north up Jalisco's Pacific coast, you will enter the small state of Nayarit, directly south of Sinaloa. Although Nayarit is small, it is one Mexico's leading tobacco growers. It also grows more varieties of fruit than any other state. The state's mountainous areas are scrubby and dry, but along the coast are fertile areas with abundant rain. The state also has two volcanoes: Ceboruco and Sanganguey.

Nayarit's capital city is Tepic. This city does not attract many tourists, but it is nevertheless known for its kindness to strangers. Many of the people who live here are very poor, and they often still wear the traditional clothing worn by their ancestors.

Although Tepic is a busy urban center, the mountains that surround it are nearly empty of people. The only residents of these high, wild areas are the Cora and Huichol Indians, who try to keep their ancient cultures intact. They venture into the towns and cities only to sell their artwork.

Tourists may not be attracted to the poverty and industrial parks of Tepic, but visitors do love Nayarit's beach towns. Nayarit's beaches lack the luxurious resorts found along other areas of Mexico's coast, but surfers, birdwatchers, and other adventuresome tourists enjoy the quieter atmosphere to be found in communities like San Blas.

COLIMA

If you leave Nayarit and once more cross Jalisco to the south, you will find yourself entering Colima. This is one of the smallest of Mexico's states, but this little area has a variety of geographical features. The beaches along the Pacific coast give way to farmland,

A bird's-eye view of Manzanillo, the main port of Colima and one of the state's most important cities.

while at the northeastern tip of the state, two volcanoes tower over the neighboring villages—and one of them is still active!

The capital city of Colima was founded in 1523 by the Spanish, and in the 1800s the city became an important stop when President Porfirio Díaz connected it by railway to the state's port city of Manzanillo. During the early 20th century, the turmoil caused by the Mexican Revolution wreaked havoc on the state of Colima, as battles raged back and forth across its fertile land. Slowly, though, the land recovered, and today its mining and shipping industries are prosperous. Tourists are also attracted to Colima's beaches and still-active volcano.

The state is a leading producer of lemons, as well as bananas, coconuts, corn, rice, and mangos. Factories are also moving into the

state, producing beverages and clothing, and new discoveries of iron ore have made Colima one of Mexico's largest iron-producing states. The port of Manzanillo has become a hub for trade with the United States, Central and South America, and countries across the Pacific Ocean.

MICHOACÁN

Heading south along the Pacific Coast from Colima brings you to the state of Michoacán. When the Aztecs ruled Mexico, the Purépeche people lived around the shores of Lake Pátzcuaro, supporting themselves on the bountiful fish that lived in the lake. As a result, the Aztecs referred to these lands as "Michoacán"—which meant "country of fishermen."

The Purépeche people spoke a language that was different from any other spoken by the native people of Mexico, and they built terraced farm plots that were also unique in the land. Today archeologists believe these people probably migrated to Mexico from the South American country of Peru.

The Purépeche lived in what is now Michoacán from about 800 B.C. until the arrival of the Spanish in their lands in 1522. European germs did their part in decreasing the Purépeche population, but today the remnants of this culture still exist. Purépeche music, dances, and art are still common in Michoacán, and the language continues to be spoken in some of the smaller villages.

Morelia, the capital city of Michoacán, is full of both colonial elegance and markets designed to appeal to tourists. The surrounding land has become a productive agricultural area. The abundant rain, mild temperatures, and rich, red soil yield enormous corn harvests.

GUERRERO

As you continue your journey south along the Pacific Coast, you will enter the state of Guerrero, home to one of Mexico's most famous cities—Acapulco. Tourism is a thriving industry in this state, as visitors from all over the world flock here to enjoy the warm weather, elegant resorts, and beautiful beaches.

Other cities like Taxco and Ixtapa also attract their share of tourists, but the pace in these smaller cities is slower than in Acapulco, and the atmosphere is gentler. Taxco is famous for its silver artisans, descendents of the original settlers who came to this city centuries ago seeking to make their fortunes in the silver mines.

Along Guerrero's coastline, the weather is often hot and steamy, but in the higher inland areas, the weather is better suited for farming. However, the tropical climate throughout much of the state means that the area's economy depends more on tourism than any other industry.

OAXACA

As you travel further along the Pacific coast you come next to the state of Oaxaca, a tropical

The city can be seen behind the cliffs of Acapulco. This important city in Guerrero is a popular tourist destination.

land that suffers from economic poverty despite its cultural riches. Until recently, this state has been ignored by tourists, and its steamy weather made farming impossible. Now, the government is working to develop resort areas that will put Oaxaca on the map, and stimulate the faltering economy.

Historically, many different groups of people—the Zapotecs, the Mixtecs, the Aztecs, and Spaniards—have fought over this land. Over the past 2,000 years, more than 200 different tribes have inhabited this region. Today, over a million of the state's inhabitants still speak some form of native language, and a fifth of the state's population does not speak any Spanish at all. The native artisans are known worldwide for their hand-woven textiles, leather goods, and pottery.

This carving of a dancer was excavated at Monte Alban, Oaxaca.

Although tourism and the state's rich mines (especially coal and iron) offer hope for the future, many of the people of Oaxaca are disillusioned with their government. So many of them are desperately poor, and in the past the government has done little to help them. As they look at the rebels in the neighboring state of Chiapas, the people of Oaxaca consider joining the fight for better conditions.

There is beautiful scenery throughout mountainous Chiapas, including the steep walls of the Canyon de Sumidero in Tuxtla Gutierrez.

CHIAPAS

Chiapas is at the tip of the Mexico Pacific coastline; if you were to continue your journey along the coast, next you would leave Mexico and enter the country of Guatemala. Until 1824, Chiapas was actually a part of Guatemala. Today, it is Mexico's poorest state.

Historically, Chiapas has always been a land of rebellion. In the 19th century, native people in the villages of Chiapas discovered *pierdras hablantes*. These "talking stones" advised the people to rebel against the Spanish, and soon the Rebellion of 1869 was underway. However, the government quickly squashed the revolt.

In the 1930s, the Mexican government began the *ejido* system, where farmland was given to communities to own jointly. This helped the people of Chiapas, but their poverty continued. By the middle of the 1990s, many farmworkers in the state were earning as little as $1.75 a day.

In 1994, Zapatista rebels occupied several towns in Chiapas, as well as Tuxtla Guitérrez, the state capital. The rebels' basic demands were for land, democratic reforms, health care, and education. When Vicente

Fox, a politician from the state of Chiapas, was elected president of Mexico in 2000, he pledged to work with the rebels and help his home state solve its many problems.

CAMPECHE

If you are going to continue your travels in Mexico, now you must leave the Pacific coast and instead turn northeast to enter the state of Campeche. Campeche's coastline is to the northwest, on the Gulf of Mexico. The economy of Campeche depends on the oil industry, since the Bay of Campeche contains many of Mexico's offshore oil fields.

Oil is not the state's only industry, though. About 14 percent of the region's economy comes from wood and wood products. Campeche's specialty is wood furniture.

The Maya once inhabited this land, and their ruins still dot the countryside. These ruins, however, tend to be smaller and more deeply hidden in the juggle than those found in Campeche's neighboring states; as a result, few tourists find their way to this state.

QUINTANA ROO

East of Campeche lies Mexico's youngest state, Quintana Roo. Many visitors insist that it is also Mexico's most beautiful region. A chain of coral reefs in the Caribbean Sea's turquoise waters guard the white beaches that stretch along the coastline. The land is filled with blue lagoons and underground caves.

Quintana Roo did not achieve statehood until the 1970s. Almost immediately, the Mexican government hit upon the idea of converting

The sun sets over the harbor at Playa del Carmen, Quintana Roo. Mexico's youngest state, Quintana Roo did not achieve statehood until the 1970s.

this tropical paradise into a tourist haven. They chose Cancún to be the center of their plan, and they worked hard to transform the city into a luxurious resort.

Their plan succeeded, and wealthy vacationers flock to Cancún every year. However, other tourists enjoy Quintana Roo's more traditional treasures—native artisans and a wealth of archeological sites. Another attraction created by the government is Sian Ka'an Biosphere Reserve, a 1.3-million-acre nature reserve that covers 10 percent of the state's land. The reserve offers lagoons, swamps, grasslands, forests, and 70 miles of coral reefs. It is home to hundreds of species of birds, fish, animals, and plants.

YUCATÁN

The other state that shares the Yucatán Peninsula with Campeche and Quintana Roo is the state of Yucatán. For years, a lack of roads and communication systems kept this state from developing, but recently the government has worked to build the *infrastructure* of this area. As tourists are able to reach the state more easily, the economy is growing. Visitors come to see the impressive Mayan ruins at Chichén Itzá and Uxmal. Tourists also enjoy the Caribbean beaches and the native handicrafts for sale in open-air markets.

Yucatán grows citrus fruit, vegetables, sisal, and cantaloupes. Beekeepers have made the state one of the world's leading honey producers. Fishing, forestry, industry, and commerce are also beginning to grow in this state.

TABASCO

To continue along Mexico's Gulf coastline, you must first cut back through the state of Campeche, in order to reach the small state of Tabasco. The name comes from the **Nahuatl** word that means "waterlogged earth." The name is appropriate, since Tabasco has almost one-third of Mexico's water resources. The state's low plains are dotted with lakes and swamps, crossed by rivers, and covered with steamy jungles. The ancient Olmecs' enormous heads are scattered through the jungles, but the state has so few rocks that the

The El Castillo pyramid is located at Chichén Itzá, Yucatán. Mayan cities like Chichén Itzá and Uxmal were major centers of the civilization.

Olmecs must have had to travel miles to get the huge pieces of stone they used to create their artwork.

Tabasco is one of Mexico's main oil-producing areas. Its growing industries produce **petrochemicals** and oil by-products. Products made from petrochemicals include plastics, soaps, fertilizer, and paint. The oil industry is bringing much-needed money to this state, but rickety shacks and shanties still cluster around the states' spreading refineries and factories.

VERACRUZ

As you journey west along the Gulf Coast, you will enter next the state of Veracruz, the first Mexican region to fall to Spanish rule when Cortés arrived on its shores. Today, the economy of this state, like Tabasco's, focuses on the oil industry. The state has more than one-fourth of Mexico's petroleum reserves; it supplies 17 percent of

Mexico's energy; and it has the nation's second largest generator and only nuclear power plant.

The discovery of oil has caused a population explosion in Veracruz. At the beginning of the 20th century, only about one million people lived in this state; now about 7 million inhabitants make this the third most populated state in Mexico.

Veracruz's fishing fleet is also the largest in Mexico, and its oyster catch is among the biggest in the country. Agriculture and manufacturing are also important parts of the state's economy, as is tourism. Visitors enjoy the many archeological sites. The southern part of the state, however, is largely undeveloped, and some tourists may find they like the slow, informal atmosphere in these small towns even better than they do some of the better known attractions. Local color is supplied by the *curanderos* (medicine men), who practice a mixture of conjuring and natural healing.

The castle of San Juan de Ulúa was built in 1528 to protect the harbor at Veracruz from Caribbean pirates. Veracruz was the first European settlement established on the American mainland; today, it is Mexico's most important seaport.

TAMAULIPAS

As you travel further along the Gulf of Mexico, you will enter the state of Tamaulipas. This states is bordered by Texas to the north, and many foreign industries are clustered along the border. American tourists enter the city of Matamoros from Brownsville, Texas. These tourists will shop for cheap Mexican trinkets and handicrafts in the many markets and stores.

Most of the residents along the border work in foreign-owned maquiladoras. Many inhabitants, however, have no work at all, and the area is full of desperate poverty. As a result, not many visitors enjoy visiting this area.

NUEVA LEÓN

Leaving the Gulf of Mexico behind and turning westward, you will enter the state of Nueva León. The state has the third largest city in Mexico, and the largest city in northern Mexico—Monterrey.

Monterrey, the state's capital city, is a community of contrasts. Modern skyscrapers tower over colonial structures; wealthy businessmen live side by side with impoverished members of the lowest class. Wooden shacks offer photocopying services to the busy workforce, and beggars hold up their hands on the steps of new, shiny banks.

COAHUILA

Continuing west brings you to the state of Coahuila. The Río Grande forms the state's northern border, with Texas on the other side of the great river. Like other border states, foreign-owned *maquiladoras* have brought both problems and hope to the people of this state.

45

The capital city of Saltillo is proud that two national heroes were born there—Venustiano Carranza, a revolutionary general called the "father of the Mexican Constitution," and Francisco Madero, the man who put an end to Porfirio Díaz's power in 1911.

The first inhabitants of the region around Saltillo were Tlaxcalteca families, people who were weavers and craftsmakers by trade. The area is still famous for its colorful *serapes*. Every year, from July 18 to August 3, visitors from all over the country and the United States come to Saltillo for culture and artistry to be found at the *Feria de Saltillo*.

SAN LUIS POTOSÍ

If you leave Coahuila by its southeastern corner, you will find yourself in the central state of San Luis Potosí. In the 1500s, silver was discovered in the state's hills of San Pedro, and settlers came to the area hoping to make a fortune. However, the silver was soon depleted; today the mines still function but mainly as tourist attractions. In Real de Catorce, visitors can visit a ghost mining town.

However, the hills of San Luis Potosí proved to be full of other minerals as well. These mines and growing dairy farms form a large part of the state's economy. The village of Santa María del Río is the state's *rebozo* capital, and visitors come from all over to buy the fine silk shawls. The streets of San Luis Potosí, the state's capital with the same name as the state, are full of *vaqueros* and Burger Kings, primitive open-air markets and elegant, baroque architecture.

Guanajuato City is the capital of Guanajuato, a Mexican cultural center.

GUANAJUATO

Crossing San Luis Potosí's southwestern border will bring you next to the state of Guanajuato. This state is part of the great, bowl-shaped *plateau* known as El Bajio. The land here is fertile and rolling, and ever since the 16th century, the area's silver mines have brought prosperity and shaped the course of its history. By the 1800s, the state supplied most of the silver that was *minted* into the country's coins. The capital city of Guanajuato became the commercial and banking center of this entire thriving region.

However, the city's wealth did little good for the ordinary people who lived there, and in the 19th century, Guanajuato was active in the Mexican fight for independence. Today, however, Guanajuato is a cultural center, sponsoring performances of drama, classical music, and ballet. Diego Rivera, the famous muralist, was born in Guanajuato, and his early works were deeply influenced by his birthplace.

QUERÉTARO

As you leave Guanajuato by crossing its eastern border, you will find yourself in Querétaro, another central state that nestles in El Bajio's fertile bowl. This small state was important in Mexican history, for here the country's current constitution was drafted. Here too the emperor Maximilian was put to death by Juárez's troops in 1867. His last words were, "Mexicans, I am going to die for a just cause: the liberty and independence of Mexico. May my blood be the last shed for the happiness of my new country!" Unfortunately, his blood was *not* the last shed for Mexico. Trouble and strife continued to haunt the nation, and the end of the Mexican-American War was finalized here as well. When Mexico signed the Treaty of Guadalupe Hidalgo in Querétero, it gave away its northern territories to the United States. Nevertheless, today Querétaro is proud of its historic past, even as it struggles to deal with the modern problems of poverty and industrial pollution.

HIDALGO

Head southeast as you leave Guanajuato, and you will find yourself in the state of Hidalgo. Shadowed by tall volcanic mountains, this area was originally inhabited by the ancient Huastec

A statue of a Spanish missionary is silhouetted against the evening sky in Querétaro City. The blending of Spanish and native cultures produced the *mestizo* culture that is dominant in Mexico today.

These statues are part of a complex built by the ancient Toltecs near the present-day city of Tula, in Hidalgo.

people. When the Toltecs rose to prominence, they built their center in what is now the city of Tula. In the end, the Toltecs were swallowed by the Aztec empire—which ultimately gave way to the Spanish in the 16th century. Then in the War for Independence, the state again suffered from heavy fighting.

But despite the centuries of turmoil, the area is now an important cog in Mexico's economic machine. Although it is often overlooked by tourists, food and precious metals flow out of the state. If you travel to Hidalgo, you can still see the ancient ruins of the Toltecs' city of Tula, outside the modern-day city. These ruins have temples, ball courts, palaces, and carved walls that depict serpents, jaguars, and eagles.

TLAXCALA

As you cross the southeastern border of Hidalgo, you enter the tiny state of Tlaxcala. The long-ago people who once lived here were the fierce enemies of the ancient Aztec city of Tenochtitlán. When Cortés arrived early in the 16th century, the Tlaxcalans were more than willing to join with his forces to fight the Aztecs they despised. King Charles V of Spain was so greatful for their help that he granted them titles of nobility.

Today, Tlaxcala is filled with reminders of both its Indian and colonial past. The town of Santa Ana Chiautempan has a 16th-century convent, while the ruins at Cacaxtla are considered to be one of Mexico's most impressive archeological sites. The massive ceremonial center was built and expanded between A.D. 600 and 750; it was abandoned in 1000. Visitors there can still see a huge detailed mural that reveals much about the beliefs and lives of the people who once lived there.

PUEBLA

If you leave Tlaxcala going any direction except northwest, you will find yourself in the state of Puebla; Puebla nearly surrounds tiny Tlaxcala. Back in the early 1500s, Cortés's conquest of Mexico began to pick up steam when he reached this area. Many local tribes from the area became allies with the Spanish, hoping to free themselves from the Aztecs' hated rule.

Some of Mexico's oldest churches are in Puebla; they were built only months after Cortés's arrival. However, if you look inside some of these churches, you will see that the Spanish conquistadors and missionaries failed to fully Christianize the native people. Images from native mythology are mixed with Christian icons, revealing the mixture of these two religions that still exists in Mexico today.

Puebla's two volcanoes, Popocatépl and Ixtaccihuatl, are the second- and third-highest mountains in the country. According to native traditions, "Popo" was a warrior who loved Ixtaccihuatl, an emperor's daughter. These star-crossed lovers remain loyal to each other, and "Popo" expresses his frustration and longing by smoking from time to time. Experienced climbers can go up to the top of both these mountains.

MORELOS

As you circle around to the northwest, you will cross the border into the state of Morelos. This small state first became a vacation spot when the Emperor Maximilian built his summer home in Cuernavaca. Thousands of other Mexicans from Mexico City followed his example, taking advantage of Cuernavaca's "eternal spring," Tepoztlán's scenic beauties, and Cuautla's swimming areas.

Today's visitors also enjoy the many archeological sites to be found in Morelos. The ancient ceremonial center at Xochicalco contains Toltec pyramids and ball courts. Tepoztlán is famous for the towering cliffs that turned this village into a natural fortress. Outside the village, perched on one of the cliffs, is yet another ancient pyramid.

MÉXICO

As you continue your circle toward the northwest, you will enter the state of México. It may seem confusing to have a state with the same name as the nation, but Mexicans seem to enjoy using their names more than once. By now, you may have noticed that many of the states' capital cities have the same name as their state. The capital city of the state of México, however, is Toluca.

This state has green plains that rise up to snow-covered mountains.

Its towns and cities are growing rapidly, as industries are drawn here to the heart of the nation. The city of Malinalco has a massive 16th-century church, as well the ruins of an Aztec temple.

MEXICO CITY, FEDERAL DISTRICT

At the very center of the circle you have been traveling is the nation's capital city, surrounded by the Federal District. It is the second largest population center in the world, with more than 20 million people living in 220 *colonias* (neighborhoods). One quarter of the country's entire population live here in the Federal District, and the area covers 522 square miles.

The city is the nation's cultural and economic center as well. Built on the foundations of the Aztecs' city of Tenochtitlán, the Federal District contains Aztec ruins, the enormous Metropolitan Cathedral, the Palace of Fine Arts, and many spectacular murals and mosaics by world-renown artists like Rivera, Orozco, and Siqueiros.

Despite its beauty, the Federal District has its problems as well, just as the rest of Mexico does. Air pollution is a growing hazard over the city's ancient foundations and modern walls; overcrowding is a real problem as well, as more and more people come to the Federal District, seeking work in the growing industrial areas; and poverty is an ever-present tragedy here, as it is throughout the rest of the country.

But like the rest of Mexico, the Federal District is full of vitality and hope. Its people use the triumphs of the past as a foundation as they struggle to build a better future.

APPENDIX: MAPS OF MEXICO

THE CENTRAL STATES OF MEXICO

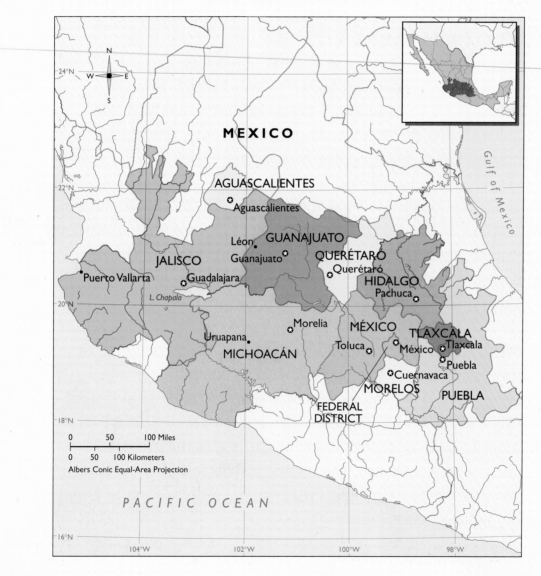

THE NORTHERN STATES OF MEXICO

STATES OF THE GULF OF MEXICO

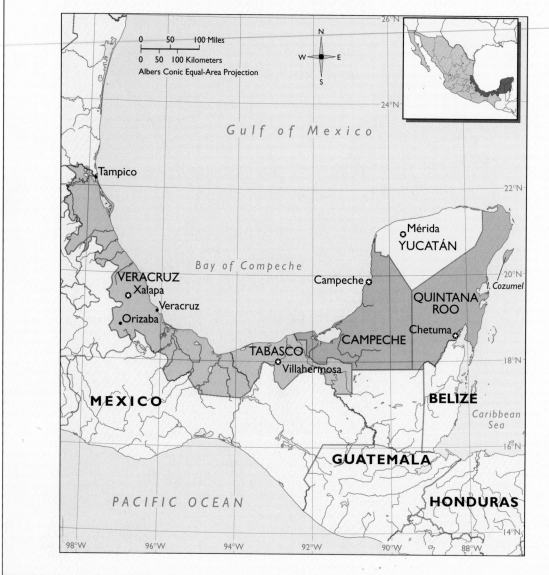

Gulf of Mexico

0   50   100 Miles
0   50   100 Kilometers
Albers Conic Equal-Area Projection

N
W   E
S

Tampico

Mérida
YUCATÁN

Bay of Compeche

VERACRUZ
Xalapa
Veracruz
Orizaba

Campeche

I. Cozumel

QUINTANA
ROO

Chetuma

CAMPECHE

TABASCO
Villahermosa

MEXICO

BELIZE

Caribbean
Sea

GUATEMALA

PACIFIC OCEAN

HONDURAS

98°W   96°W   94°W   92°W   90°W   88°W

26°N
24°N
22°N
20°N
18°N
16°N
14°N

54

STATES OF THE PACIFIC NORTH OF MEXICO

55

STATES OF THE PACIFIC SOUTH OF MEXICO

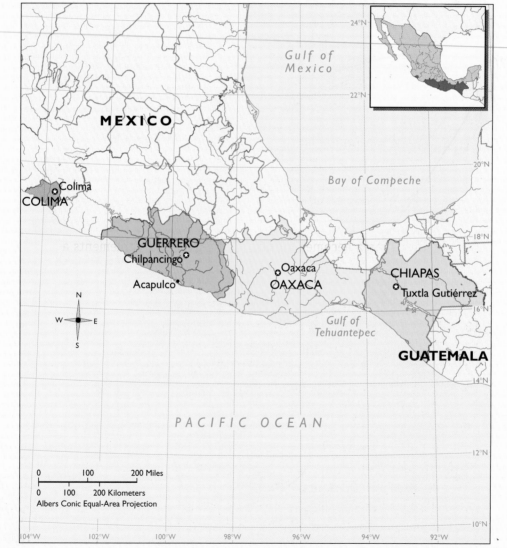

Gulf of
Mexico

24°N

22°N

MEXICO

20°N

Bay of Compeche

Colima

COLIMA

GUERRERO

18°N

Chilpancingo

Oaxaca

OAXACA

CHIAPAS

Tuxtla Gutiérrez

Acapulco

16°N

N

W   E

S

Gulf of
Tehuantepec

GUATEMALA

14°N

PACIFIC OCEAN

12°N

0   100   200 Miles

0   100   200 Kilometers

Albers Conic Equal-Area Projection

10°N

104°W   102°W   100°W   98°W   96°W   94°W   92°W

CHRONOLOGY

1000 B.C. The Olmec civilization becomes a leader in development of writing, numbering, and astronomy.

400 B.C. Olmec civilization disappears.

150 B.C. Teotihuacán is built.

A.D. 750 Teotihuacán is abandoned.

300–900 Peak cultural growth of the Maya.

1325 Aztecs build Tenochtitlán.

1519 Hernán Cortés arrives in Mexico.

1521 Spanish take control of Mexico.

1810 Father Miguel Hidalgo calls for Mexico's independence from Spain.

1821 Mexico wins its independence.

1836 Texas is granted independence from Spain in the Velasco Agreement.

1845 United States invites Texas to join the union, sparking the Mexican-American War.

1854 Benito Juárez becomes president of Mexico and implements a period of reform.

1862 France invades Mexico.

1867 Juárez triumphs over the French and resumes his presidency.

1876 Porfirio Díaz begins his period of dictatorship.

1910 The Mexican Revolution begins.

1921 The end of the Revolution and the beginning of modern-day Mexico.

1968 Mexico hosts the Summer Olympic Games, and violence breaks out during a student protest.

2000 Vicente Fox becomes the first president in over 70 years who is not a member of the PRI.

2001 President Fox visits the White House to meet with President George W. Bush of the United States.

2002 Mexico's Vicente Fox meets with other Latin American leaders in Argentina for the Global Alumni Conference.

57

FURTHER READING

Carew-Miller, Anna. *Famous People of Mexico*. Philadelphia: Mason Crest Publishers, 2003.

Fehrenbach, T. R. *Fire and Blood, a History of Mexico*. New York: Da Capo Press, 1995.

Franz, Carl. *The People's Guide to Mexico*. Emeryville, Calif.: Publishers Group West, 1995.

Goodwin, William. *Mexico: Modern Nations of the World*. San Diego: Lucent Press, 1999.

Hunter, Amy N. *The History of Mexico*. Philadelphia: Mason Crest Publishers, 2003.

Kimmel, Eric A. *Montezuma and the Fall of the Aztecs*. New York: Holiday House, 2000.

O'Reilly, James and Larry Habegger. *Travelers' Tales: Mexico*. Sebastopol, Calif.: Travelers' Tales, 1994.

Rummel, Jack. *Mexico*. Philadelphia: Chelsea House Publishers, 1999.

Warburton, Lois. *World History Series—Aztec Civilization*. San Diego: Lucent Press, 1995.

Werner, Michael. *The History of Mexico: History, Culture, and Society*. Chicago: Fitzroy Dearborn Publishers, 1997.

Williams, Colleen Madonna Flood. *The Geography of Mexico*. Philadelphia: Mason Crest Publishers, 2003.

INTERNET RESOURCES

Visiting Mexico
www.elbalero.gob.mx/pages_kids/
geography/geography_kids.html

www.nationalgeographic.com/mexico/

www.inegi.gob.mx/diffusion/ingles/
portadai.html

www.dizzy.library.arizona.edu.

www.cababob.baja.com

www.tourbymexico.com

Festivals and Celebrations
www.mexicanculture.about.com/
culture/mexicanculture/mbody.htm

www.mexonline.com/history.htm

www.theodora.com/wfb/
mexico_people.html

www.mexconnect.com

www.angelfire.com/ca5/mexhistory/

www.mesoweb.com/
welcome.html#externalresources

www.elbalero.gob.mx/index_kids.html

www.uapress.arizona.edu/online.bks/s
eris/history.htm

Government and Economy
www.odci.gov/cia/publications/
factbook/geos/mx.html

www.behindthelabel.org

www.mexicolaw.com

Sports and Entertainment
www.bullfights.org/faq/index.shtml

www.wspa.org.uk/campaigns/
bullfighting/mexico.html

www.tsha.utexas.edu/handbook/
online/articles/view/CC/llc4.html

www.mexconnect.com/mex_/bull.html

www.edunetconnect.com/cat/games/
handball.html

www.geocities.com/Colosseum/
Sideline/7480/index1.htm

www.mexicochannel.net

History
www.go2mexico.com/article/history/

www.mexconnect.com/mex_/history/
historyindex.html

lanic.utexas.edu/la/Mexico

Art and Architecture
www.nmwa.org/legacy/bios/bkahlo.htm

www.mexconnect.com

www.mexonline.com/history.htm

www.lanic.utexas.edu/la/Mexico

www.dartmouth.edu/~sorjuana

www.diegorivera.com/
diego_home_eng.html

59

GLOSSARY

Baroque	An ornate style of art and architecture popular during the 17th century.
Catacombs	A network of underground passages or tunnels, sometimes used as a burial site.
Conquistadors	The Spanish conquerors of the New World.
Export	To ship a product out of a country to markets in other nations.
Fiesta	A Mexican celebration or party.
Haciendas	Spanish ranches.
Hat dance	A traditional Mexican dance.
Illiteracy	The inability to read or write.
Immigrate	To move one's residence from one nation or area to another.
Immunities	The natural abilities to resist diseases.
Import	To bring a product into a country from another nation.
Inflation	A rise in prices.
Infrastructure	A nation's system of public works, such as roads, railways, and schools.
Lagoon	Body of water that is connected to a sea or bay.
Mariachis	Mexican street bands.
Mennonites	Members of a Protestant religious group who believe in pacifism and sometime isolate themselves from the influences of modern society.
Migrating	Traveling from one area to another.
Minted	Shaped metal into coins.
Murals	Large pictures painted on walls.

Nahuatl — The language spoken by the Aztecs, still spoken by many people in Mexico today.

Peso — Mexico's unit of money.

Petrochemicals — Chemicals derived from oil.

Plateau — High, flat land.

Rebozo — A long scarf worn by Mexican women.

Reclamation — Taking back; making something useable once more.

Serapes — Colorful woolen shawls worn over the shoulders by Mexican men.

Smallpox — A contagious disease that causes high fever and pus-filled sores that leave deep scars.

Tropical — The region to the north and south of the equator, which is very hot and often has a high level of humidity.

Vaqueros — Mexican cowboys.

INDEX

63

PICTURE CREDITS

CONTRIBUTORS

Roger E. Hernández is the most widely syndicated columnist writing on Hispanic issues in the United States. His weekly column, distributed by King Features, appears in some 40 newspapers across the country, including the *Washington Post*, *Los Angeles Daily News*, *Dallas Morning News*, *Arizona Republic*, *Rocky Mountain News* in Denver, *El Paso Times*, and *Hartford Courant*. He is also the author of *Cubans in America*, an illustrated history of the Cuban presence in what is now the United States, from the early colonists in 16th-century Florida to today's Castro-era exiles. The book was designed to accompany a PBS documentary of the same title.

Hernández's articles and essays have been published in the *New York Times*, *New Jersey Monthly*, *Reader's Digest*, and *Vista Magazine*; he is a frequent guest on television and radio political talk shows, and often travels the country to lecture on his topic of expertise. Currently, he is teaching journalism and English composition at the New Jersey Institute of Technology in Newark, where he holds the position of writer-in-residence. He is also a member of the adjunct faculty at Rutgers University.

Hernández left Cuba with his parents at the age of nine. After living in Spain for a year, the family settled in Union City, New Jersey, where Hernandez grew up. He attended Rutgers University, where he earned a BA in Journalism in 1977; after graduation, he worked in television news before moving to print journalism in 1983. He lives with his wife and two children in Upper Montclair, New Jersey.

Ellyn Sanna has authored more than 50 books, including adult nonfiction, novels, young adult biographies, and gift books. She also works as a freelance editor and helps take care of three children, a cat, a rabbit, a one-eyed hamster, two hermit crabs, and a goldfish.

17